Lerner SPORTS

WNBA Hot Ticket

MINNESOTA LYNX

JOSH ANDERSON

Lerner Publications ◆ Minneapolis

To Leo and Dane, the biggest superstars I've ever met.

The stats and information in this book are accurate through the 2024 WNBA season.

Lerner Publications Company
An imprint of Lerner Publishing Group, Inc.
241 First Avenue North
Minneapolis, MN 55401 USA

For reading levels and more information, look up this title at www.lernerbooks.com.

Main body text set in Aptifer Slab LT Pro / Typeface provided by Linotype AG

Library of Congress Cataloging-in-Publication Data

Names: Anderson, Josh, author.
Title: Minnesota Lynx / Josh Anderson.
Description: Minneapolis, MN : Lerner Publications, [2026] | Series: Wnba hot ticket (Lerner sports) | Includes bibliographical references and index. | Audience: Ages 7–11 | Audience: Grades 2–3 | Summary: "With four championships, no WNBA team has had more success than the Minnesota Lynx. From legends such as Maya Moore to modern superstar Napheesa Collier, meet the players and relive the greatest Lynx moments"—Provided by publisher.
Identifiers: LCCN 2024046189 (print) | LCCN 2024046190 (ebook) | ISBN 9798765670088 (library binding) | ISBN 9798765683569 (paperback) | ISBN 9798765682050 (epub)
Subjects: LCSH: Minnesota Lynx (Basketball team)—History—Juvenile literature. | Basketball for women—United States—Juvenile literature. | Women basketball players—United States—Biography—Juvenile literature. | Basketball players—United States—Biography—Juvenile literature.
Classification: LCC GV885.52.M563 A53 2026 (print) | LCC GV885.52.M563 (ebook) | DDC 796.323/6409776—dc23/eng/20241231

LC record available at https://lccn.loc.gov/2024046189
LC ebook record available at https://lccn.loc.gov/2024046190

Manufactured in the United States of America
1 - CG - 7/15/25

TABLE OF CONTENTS

Nneka Ogwumike (*left*) of the Los Angeles Sparks battles Minnesota Lynx center Sylvia Fowles (*right*) in Game 5 of the 2017 WNBA Finals.

A FOURTH TITLE

FACTS AT A GLANCE

- The Minnesota Lynx tied the Women's National Basketball Association (WNBA) record by winning their **FOURTH CHAMPIONSHIP** in 2017.
- The team picked **MAYA MOORE** first overall in the 2011 WNBA Draft.
- Center **SYLVIA FOWLES** is the WNBA's all-time leader in rebounds.
- Head coach **CHERYL REEVE** joined the Lynx in 2010 and finished her 15th season with the team in 2024.

The Minnesota Lynx were close to making history in the WNBA. Only one team had won four championships since the league began in 1997. If the Lynx could hold on to their lead, they'd become the second.

Minnesota was ahead throughout the fourth quarter of Game 5 of the 2017 WNBA Finals. But with 34 seconds left in the game, Los Angeles Sparks guard Odyssey Sims hit a layup and was fouled. Sims's free throw brought the Sparks to within three points, 79–76. The Lynx needed a basket to secure the win.

Every Lynx fan inside Minnesota's Williams Arena knew who should get the ball. Minnesota forward Maya Moore and center Sylvia Fowles were the team's top targets. The ball went to Moore, who had been the Most Valuable Player (MVP) of the 2013 Finals.

Moore dribbled toward the basket from outside the three-point line. She stopped just behind the free-throw line and floated a shot toward the hoop. It fell through the net, giving the Lynx an 81–76 lead.

The Sparks took the ball down the court and missed a three-point attempt. Fowles grabbed her 20th rebound of the game, setting a WNBA Finals record. The Sparks were forced to foul to stop the clock. Lynx players hit four free throws in the final seconds, and Minnesota won the game 85–76.

It was the fourth WNBA title in seven years for the Lynx. They were tied with the Houston Comets as the only WNBA teams to win the championship four times. The Seattle Storm would also win their fourth title a few years later. But the Lynx were the only pro sports team in the United States to win four titles in the 2010s.

Lynx players celebrate their fourth WNBA title after defeating the Los Angeles Sparks.

Maya Moore (*left*) and Seimone Augustus (*right*) combined for 143 points during the 2017 Finals.

Katie Smith (*left*) started her career with the Lynx and played almost seven seasons with the team.

CHAPTER 1

BEST IN THE LEAGUE

The Minnesota Lynx began play during the WNBA's third season in 1999 as an expansion team. The Orlando Miracle were also added to the league that season. The Miracle later moved to Connecticut and became the Connecticut Sun. The Lynx are named after an animal that lives in Minnesota. Lynx are wildcats found throughout the northern United States and Canada.

The Lynx are the only WNBA team named after an animal. Minnesota's National Basketball Association team, the Timberwolves, are also named after an animal.

Like many expansion teams, the Lynx lost more than they won during their first few seasons. The team's best player in its early years was guard Katie Smith. She helped lead the Lynx to the playoffs during her last two full seasons in Minnesota in 2003 and 2004. Those seasons were the Lynx's only playoff appearances during the team's first 12 years.

In 2006, the Lynx chose first overall in the WNBA Draft. They picked Seimone Augustus, who would play 14 seasons for the team. In 2010, the Lynx traded for All-Star guard Lindsay Whalen and hired head coach Cheryl Reeve. Whalen and Reeve were two more building blocks for success.

Lindsay Whalen (*right*) dribbles past a Connecticut Sun defender during a 2010 game.

Coach Cheryl Reeve (*left*) instructs Lindsay Whalen (*center*) and Maya Moore (*right*) during a time-out.

After finishing with a disappointing 13–21 record in 2010, the Lynx again picked first overall in the WNBA Draft. This time, they chose University of Connecticut (UConn) star Maya Moore. With Moore onboard, the team improved quickly. After finishing near the bottom of the league the year before, the Lynx finished with the WNBA's best record in 2011. They ended their incredible season by defeating the Atlanta Dream in the WNBA Finals. The 2011 championship marked the beginning of an incredible period for the team.

HOOPS SCOOP

In 2014, Maya Moore became the first WNBA MVP in team history.

Lynx players celebrate their win in the 2015 WNBA Finals.

The Lynx made it to the Finals again in 2012, this time losing to the Indiana Fever. Then, in a Finals rematch with the Atlanta Dream, the Lynx won the title again in 2013. The Lynx avenged their loss from three years earlier by defeating the Fever in the 2015 Finals. And after losing the Finals in 2016, the Lynx won their fourth title in 2017 when they defeated the Sparks.

Minnesota has made the playoffs six times since their 2017 title, but the team is still searching for their fifth championship. Luckily, the Lynx have one of the league's best players in forward Napheesa Collier, a four-time All-Star who can dominate on both offense and defense.

CHANGEMAKERS

The Lynx want to help girls and women be seen and heard in Minnesota, both in sports and in their communities. One of the ways the team does this is through their Changemakers program. The program's goal is to help girls grow into leaders and raise awareness for women's sports in Minnesota. In 2024, the team held its first Changemakers Summit. Former Lynx star Maya Moore and others talked about ways the team and its community partners could impact and improve the lives of girls in the area.

The Changemakers program allows players to make a difference for young athletes in the community.

Katie Smith scored 3,605 points during her seven seasons with the Lynx. Smith became part of the team's coaching staff in 2020.

CHAPTER 2

AMAZING STARS

Katie Smith was Minnesota's star during the team's early years. She played nearly seven seasons for the team and helped lead the Lynx to the playoffs twice. Smith ranks third in league history with 906 three-pointers. She is 11th in career points with 6,452.

Playing 14 of her 15 WNBA seasons for the Lynx, Seimone Augustus played in more games for the team than any other player. She is the team's leading scorer with 5,881 points. Augustus was part of all four Lynx championship teams. She's a member of the Basketball Hall of Fame.

Seimone Augustus (*center*) shoots over two Los Angeles Sparks defenders during the 2016 Finals.

Head coach Cheryl Reeve took over the team one season before Minnesota's incredible run of six Finals appearances and four titles in seven seasons. Reeve is one of only two WNBA coaches to win four championships. She won the WNBA's Coach of the Year award in 2011, 2016, and 2020. In 2024, Reeve led the USA Basketball Women's National Team to their 10th gold medal at the Olympic Games. It was Reeve's first Olympic win as head coach.

Cheryl Reeve became head coach of the USA Basketball Women's National Team in 2021. She led the team to a gold medal in the 2024 Olympics.

Lindsay Whalen won gold medals at the 2012 and 2016 Olympics as part of the USA Basketball Women's National Team.

Guard Lindsay Whalen was born and raised in Minnesota. She attended college and played basketball at the University of Minnesota. After playing the early seasons of her WNBA career for the Connecticut Sun, Whalen went home to Minnesota in a 2010 trade. She was an All-Star four times in her nine seasons with the Lynx and was a part of all four championship teams. After her playing career, Whalen became a member of the Basketball Hall of Fame. In 2024, Whalen returned to the Lynx as an assistant coach.

Maya Moore's eight-season WNBA career could be described as nearly perfect. Averaging more than 18 points per game for the Lynx, Moore led the team to four WNBA titles. She was the league's MVP in 2014 and finished second for the award two other times. Moore was an All-Star six times. At the age of 29, Moore left the WNBA to focus on social justice.

Maya Moore averaged a career-high 23.9 points per game during the 2014 season.

HOOPS SCOOP

Maya Moore is the team's all-time leader with 451 steals.

The Lynx retired Maya Moore's number 23 after a 2024 game. In her honor, no Lynx player can wear 23 in the future.

HOOPS SCOOP

While still playing for the Lynx, Lindsay Whalen became head coach of the University of Minnesota Golden Gophers women's basketball team. She retired from playing at the end of the 2018 season and continued coaching the Golden Gophers until 2023.

Sylvia Fowles (*right*) battles with Las Vegas Aces star A'ja Wilson (*left*) for a rebound during a 2018 game.

After playing seven seasons for the Chicago Sky, Sylvia Fowles came to the Lynx in 2015. She played eight seasons for the team until her retirement in 2022. Fowles was part of two WNBA championship teams with the Lynx.

Fowles helped the team win through her scoring, rebounding, and defense. She was the Finals MVP in both 2015 and 2017 and the WNBA MVP in 2017. Fowles ranks second in league history with 4,006 career rebounds. She also won four gold medals as a member of the USA Basketball Women's National Team.

Sylvia Fowles (*left*) was the WNBA's top rebounder in 2013, 2018, and 2021.

Lynx guard Anna Cruz calls out instructions to her teammates as she dribbles down the court during the 2015 Finals.

CHAPTER 3

BUZZER-BEATER

The Lynx and Indiana Fever had split the first two games of the 2015 WNBA Finals. The first team to win three games in the series would become league champions. When the teams took the court for Game 3 in Indiana, every player knew that a win would put them one game away from a WNBA title.

Game 3 was close. Neither team could build a lead of more than seven points. With about two minutes left in the fourth quarter, the Fever's Briann January hit a jump shot that excited the Indiana crowd and gave the Fever a 77–74 lead.

Lynx and Fever players fight for the ball during a close Game 3 in the 2015 Finals.

With just over a minute remaining in the game, Lynx guard Anna Cruz drove toward the basket. She passed the ball to teammate Renee Montgomery, who was standing outside the three-point line. Montgomery didn't hesitate. She launched a three-pointer that fell through the net. The Lynx and Fever were tied 77–77.

With four seconds left, the Fever's Shenise Johnson missed a three-point shot. In a scramble for the rebound, the ball went out of bounds. The ball would belong to Minnesota with 1.7 seconds left and the score still tied.

Lindsay Whalen grabbed 21 rebounds and logged 33 assists during the 2015 playoffs.

In her eight-year WNBA career, Maya Moore (*left*) averaged 19.2 points per game in the playoffs and won four championships. Her game-winning shot during the 2015 Finals is a top moment in Lynx history.

After a time-out, point guard Lindsay Whalen stood out of bounds, looking for someone to pass to. Lynx star Maya Moore ran back and forth, trying to get away from Fever defender Marissa Coleman. Whalen lofted a pass to Moore in the middle of the court behind the three-point line. Moore faked a shot, and Coleman jumped to try to block it. Moore dribbled once to her right and took a shot with less than a second left on the game clock.

As the basketball spun through the air, the buzzer sounded to signal time had run out. Since Moore's shot was released with time left, it would count if the ball went into the basket. As players, coaches, and fans watched, the ball fell through the net. Lynx players celebrated their win on the court. The Lynx went on to win the series in five games. They had won their third of four championships during the team's incredible seven-year run.

Lynx players celebrate another big win.

CHAPTER 4

THE RACE TO FIVE

The Lynx picked Napheesa Collier in the first round of the 2019 WNBA Draft. Like Lynx legend Maya Moore, Collier also played college basketball at UConn. Collier won the WNBA Rookie of the Year award in 2019 and was an All-Star in her first season. Since then, she has been part of three other All-Star teams. Collier has ranked among the WNBA's leaders in points, rebounds, steals, and blocks since coming into the league. In 2024, she won the WNBA Defensive Player of the Year award.

The team's other top player is Kayla McBride. McBride joined the Lynx in 2021. Halfway through the 2024 season, McBride became only the 10th player in WNBA history to make 600 or more three-point shots in her career. She did it in just 326 games, making her the third-fastest player to do so.

In her first six seasons with the Lynx, Napheesa Collier averaged 17.4 points and 7.9 rebounds per game.

The Houston Comets stopped playing after the 2008 WNBA season. That leaves the Lynx in a race with the Seattle Storm. The goal is to become the first team in league history to win five WNBA titles. The Lynx came close in 2024. They lost in the Finals to the New York Liberty in five thrilling games.

The WNBA is more popular than it has ever been. There is more talent throughout the league than ever before. Coach Cheryl Reeve is confident that there's enough talent on her roster for the Lynx to win a historic fifth title.

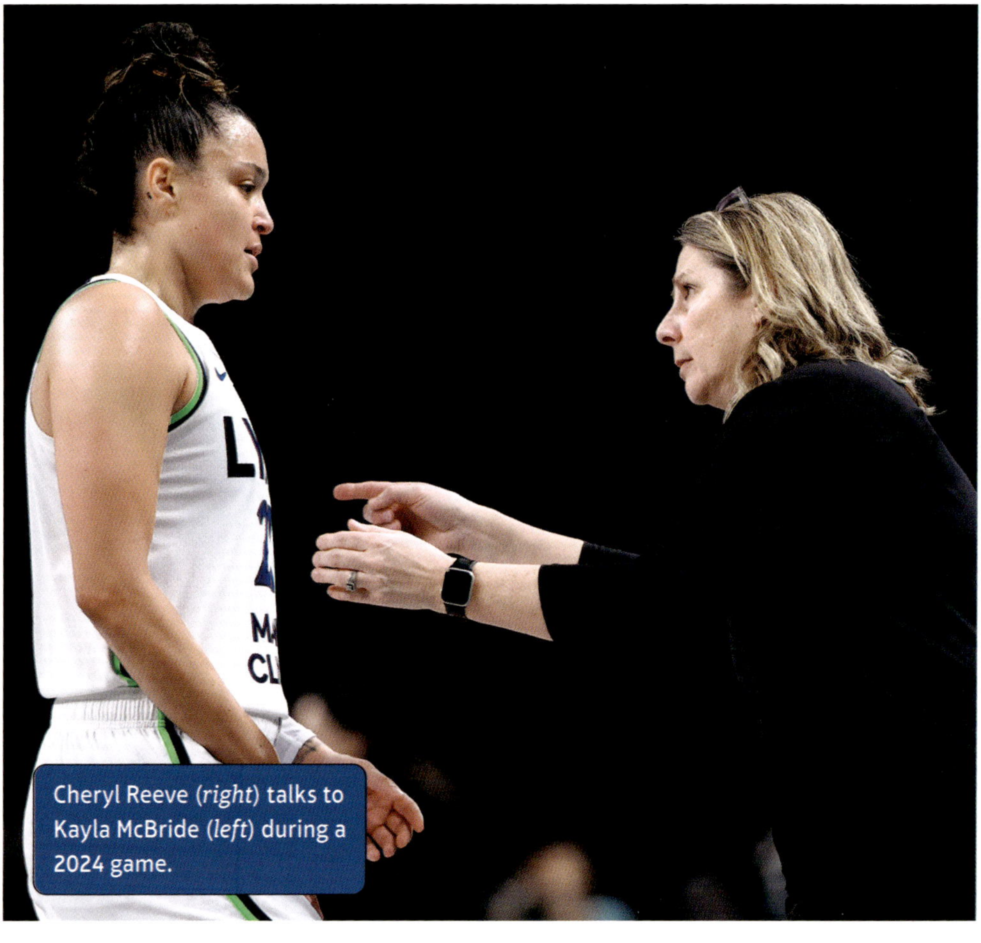

Cheryl Reeve (*right*) talks to Kayla McBride (*left*) during a 2024 game.

Napheesa Collier is one of the top players in the WNBA and gives the Lynx the edge they need to win another WNBA title.

GLOSSARY

All-Star: a player chosen as one of the best in league to compete in a game against other top players

Basketball Hall of Fame: a museum in Springfield, Massachusetts, that honors basketball's greatest coaches and players

expansion team: a team added to an existing sports league

free throw: an open shot taken from behind a set line after a foul by an opponent

layup: a shot made from near the basket usually by playing the ball off the backboard

playoffs: games held after the season to determine each year's champion

rebound: grabbing and controlling the ball after a missed shot

rookie: a first-year player

roster: a list of players on a team

WNBA Draft: when WNBA teams take turns choosing new players

WNBA Finals: the WNBA's championship series

LEARN MORE

Doeden, Matt. *G.O.A.T. Women's Basketball Teams.* Minneapolis: Lerner Publications, 2021.

Mahoney, Brian. *GOATs of Basketball.* Minneapolis: Abdo Publishing, 2022.

Whiting, Jim. *The Story of the Minnesota Lynx.* Mankato, MN: Creative Education and Creative Paperbacks, 2024.

Minnesota Lynx
https://lynx.wnba.com/

WNBA
https://www.wnba.com/

Women's National Basketball Association Facts for Kids
https://kids.kiddle.co/Women%27s_National_Basketball_Association

INDEX

PHOTO ACKNOWLEDGMENTS

Image credits: Hannah Foslien/Getty Images, p.4; Hannah Foslien/Getty Images, p.6; Hannah Foslien/Getty Images, p.7; Bruce Bisping/Star Tribune via Getty Images, p.8; David Berding/Getty Images, p. 9; David Brewster/ Star Tribune via Getty Images, p.10; Kevin C. Cox/Getty Images, p.11; Hannah Foslien/Getty Images, p.12; Erica Denhoff/Icon Sportswire via Getty Images, p.13; Marlin Levison/Star Tribune via Getty Images, p.14; Harry How/Getty Images, p.15; David Berding/Getty Images, p.16; M. Anthony Nesmith/ Icon Sportswire via Getty Images, p.17; Hannah Foslien/Getty Images, p.18; Ben Brewer/Getty Images, p.19; Sam Wasson/Getty Images, p.20; Kevork Djansezian/Getty Images, p.21; Andy Lyons/Getty Images, p.22; Kyndell Harkness/ZUMA Press/Newscom, p.23; Andy Lyons/Getty Images, p.24; Michael Hickey/Getty Images, p.25; Andy Lyons/Getty Images, p.26; Stephen Maturen/Getty Images, p.27; Dustin Satloff/Getty Images, p.28; Ben Brewer/ Getty Images, p. 29

Cover image: Tony Gutierrez/AP Photo